Games Around the World

Juggling

by Elizabeth Dana Jaffe

Content Adviser: Mark Bakalor, Professional juggler
Social Science Adviser: Professor Sherry L. Field, Department of Curriculum and Instruction, College of Education, The University of Texas at Austin
Reading Adviser: Dr. Linda D. Labbo, Department of Reading Education, College of Education, The University of Georgia

COMPASS POINT BOOKS
MINNEAPOLIS, MINNESOTA

Compass Point Books
3722 West 50th Street, #115
Minneapolis, MN 55410

Visit Compass Point Books on the Internet at *www.compasspointbooks.com* or e-mail your request to
custserv@compasspointbooks.com

Photographs ©: Gregg Andersen, cover, 5; Dean Conger/Corbis, 4; North Wind Picture Archives, 6;
Giraudon/Art Resource, N.Y., 7; Underwood & Underwood/Corbis, 8; Hulton-Deutsch Collection/Corbis, 9;
Unicorn Stock Photos/David Cummings, 11; AFP/Corbis, 13; Catherine Karnow/Corbis, 26;
Unicorn Stock Photos/Louie Bunde, 27.

Editors: E. Russell Primm and Emily J. Dolbear
Photo Researchers: Svetlana Zhurkina and Jo Miller
Photo Selector: Emily J. Dolbear
Designer: Bradfordesign, Inc.
Illustrator: Brandon Reibeling

Library of Congress Cataloging-in-Publication Data

Jaffe, Elizabeth Dana.
    Juggling / by Elizabeth D. Jaffe.
       p. cm. — (Games around the world)
    Includes bibliographical references.
    Summary: Provides a history of juggling and instructions for performing several juggling
    tricks as performed in the United States, China, and Israel.
    ISBN 0-7565-0191-1 (hardcover)
       1. Juggling—Juvenile literature. [1. Juggling.] I. Title. II. Series.
    GV1558 .J34 2002
    793.8'7—dc21   2001004746

Table of Contents

Up in the Air

Start by tossing one small ball into the air. Then toss another ball. Now toss a third ball into the air. Can you keep tossing and catching the balls without dropping any of them? If you can, you are **juggling!**

Master jugglers throw knives, hoops, sticks, and clubs. Some expert jugglers can keep tables, bowling balls, chain saws, and even people moving in the air.

At first, juggling may seem difficult. With lots of practice and patience, however, it becomes easy. Once you learn, you will never forget how to juggle. It's like riding a bike!

▲ *Beanbags for juggling*

◀ *Two performers in Beijing, China, juggle tables with their feet.*

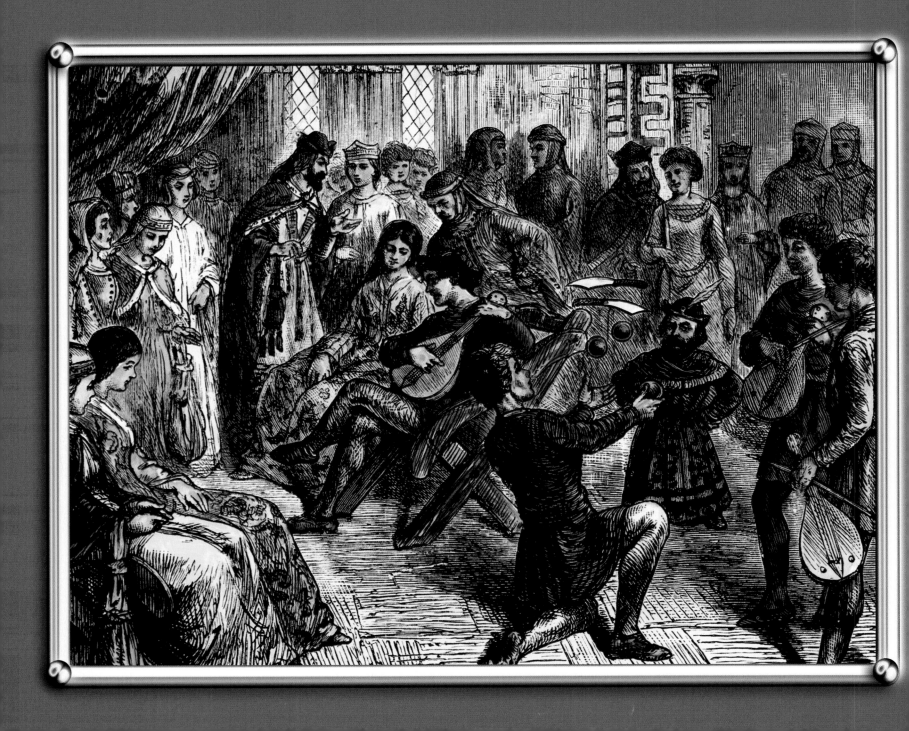

The History of Juggling

Juggling has been popular for thousands of years. People juggled in ancient Egypt, Rome, and Greece. Wall paintings of jugglers near the Nile River in Egypt may date back to 1900 B.C.

People have juggled in many other countries around the world, too. Jugglers performed in China, Japan, Iran, India, Mexico, and the United States. Native Americans also juggled.

For a long time, juggling was a special skill. Jugglers were often part of religious events.

In the 1500s, entertainers called jesters knew how to juggle. Jesters entertained kings and queens. They did tricks, told jokes, and juggled.

▲ A stone carving of a Roman juggler from the first century

◄ In the 1500s, jesters often juggled to entertain kings and queens.

Jesters also traveled to festivals, fairs, and town squares to do their acts for the public.

In the following 400 years, only a few people mastered the art of juggling. They performed mostly with traveling circuses.

Then, in the beginning of the 1900s, juggling became popular again in Europe and America. Skilled jugglers attracted big crowds. People also learned to juggle just for fun.

One of the greatest jugglers of all time was from Italy. His name was Enrico Rastelli. Both his parents

In 1936, schoolchildren learn to juggle in Ilford, England. ▶

worked in the circus.
As a young boy, Enrico
loved juggling. He often
practiced twelve hours
a day.

Why Is It Called Juggling?
The word *juggler* comes from the Latin word *joculare. Joculare* means "to joke."

The great Enrico Rastelli juggled balls, sticks, and plates. In one routine, Enrico could juggle seven balls, twirl three rings on one leg, and spin balls on a mouth-piece—all at the same time. He did this balancing on a board on a rolling tube!

Jugglers today work in many different ways. Each juggler brings his or her personality to the act.

Some jugglers work alone. Some juggle with other people. Many people juggle with their hands. Others juggle with their feet or with their legs.

Some people juggle while they are standing on a moving horse or riding a unicycle. Others juggle strange or heavy objects, such as top hats, flaming torches, or cannon-balls. Some jugglers tell stories or sing while they perform. The ways people juggle are endless!

▲ A performer juggles with fire!

How to Practice

To learn to juggle, you will need to practice. You will also need lots of patience.

When you practice, you can expect to drop the objects, or **props**, a lot. It helps to stand in front of a couch or a bed against the wall.

Make sure the props you juggle won't bounce much. Use small balls or beanbags. Then you won't have to chase after the props when you drop them. You could also try juggling nylon scarves.

Make Your Own Juggling Balls

If you don't have any beanbags, try making your own juggling balls. All you need are some coins and three old socks. Pick thin socks. Put a few coins into one sock. Tie it off. Turn the sock inside out and knot it again. Turn it inside out. Now it's a juggling ball. Make two more and start juggling!

▲ *Chinese performers spin plates on sticks.*

They float gently to the ground.

When a prop hits the floor, the wall, or anything else, it's called a **drop**. The tosses and catches you make before the drop are called a **run**. You will probably have a lot of drops before you get a run!

There are many kinds of juggling. Balancing a stick or ball on the body is one way to juggle. Spinning a ball is also a kind of juggling. Spinning plates is the Chinese form of juggling.

Juggling Do's and Don'ts

- Practice in a room that has nothing breakable in it.

- Expect to look silly when you start practicing. You might want to practice alone.

- Use the same balls each time. That will help you develop good timing.

- At first, don't practice too much each day. You might feel discouraged—and you will certainly feel sore!

- Don't toss the balls too high.

- Don't move your body to catch the balls. Keep your feet in the same comfortable position.

The Basic Beanbag Juggle

The best way to learn to juggle is to start simply. For example, start with one beanbag. When you are ready, add the second beanbag. With practice, you'll be juggling three beanbags!

What you need: Three small beanbags

How to juggle one beanbag:

1.   Stand comfortably. Put your two hands—palms up—in front of your waist.

2.   Cup a beanbag in one hand.

3.   Toss the beanbag into the air. Don't toss it higher than your eye level, though.

▲ *Stand with your hands out.*

15

The beanbag should make an arc and start to fall. Keep your eyes on the top of the arc of each throw.

4. Catch the beanbag with your other hand as it comes down.

5. Now toss the beanbag to the other hand in the same way.

6. Do this back and forth between your left and right hands.

7. Practice throwing the beanbag to the same place each time. Always remember to let the beanbag come to you.

8. Practice!

▲ *Don't toss the beanbag any higher than eye level.*

How to juggle two beanbags:

1. You will need a second beanbag.

2. Make sure you are standing comfortably. Put your two hands—palms up—in front of your waist.

3. Cup one beanbag in each hand.

4. Toss up the first beanbag gently.

5. Just as the first beanbag hits the top of its arc, throw the second

▲ *Cup one beanbag in each hand.*

beanbag up. Remember to toss the bean-bag up—not across your body.

6. Catch the first beanbag as it drops down into your other hand.

7. When the second beanbag hits the top of its arc, toss the first beanbag up again.

8. Now catch the second beanbag as it drops.

9. Continue the toss-and-catch **pattern**. Remember that each new toss should be just under the arc of the ball you already tossed.

10. Practice! Practice!

▲ *Toss the first beanbag up again when the other bean-bag is at the top of its arc.*

How to juggle three beanbags:

1. You will need a third beanbag.

2. Make sure you are standing comfortably. Put your two hands—palms up—in front of your waist.

3. Cup two beanbags in one hand. Cup the third beanbag in the other hand.

4. Toss the first beanbag into the air. As the first beanbag hits the top of its arc, toss the second beanbag just under the arc of the first beanbag. Then catch the first beanbag.

▲ *Are you ready to juggle three beanbags?*

19

5. When the second beanbag hits the top of its arc, toss the third beanbag. Now catch the second beanbag.

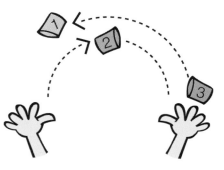

6. When the third beanbag hits the top of its arc, toss the first beanbag up again. Then catch the third beanbag.

7. Toss the second beanbag when the first beanbag hits the top of its arc. Then catch the first beanbag.

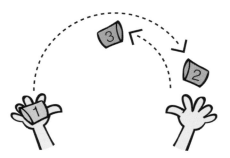

8. Remember—only two beanbags are in the air at the same time.

9. Try to continue the pattern as long as you can. See how long a run you can have.

▲ *When you juggle three beanbags, only two are in the air at once.*

10. Practice! Practice! Practice!

Spinning Plates

People in China have enjoyed spinning plates for hundreds of years. Jugglers spin plates on thin rods called **handsticks**. Chinese props are often shaped like birds, fish, or other animals. The movements sometimes look like a pair of flapping wings or a wagging tail. Spinning plates may look difficult, but anyone can learn. There are several ways to spin a plate.

What you need: A thin wooden stick about 3 feet (90 centimeters) long, and a plastic plate with a lip on the bottom and a dimple in the middle. (You will probably have to buy or borrow a simple juggling set with this special plate.)

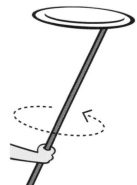

How to spin a plate with a hand start:

1. Hold the handstick in the middle. Point it straight up. The top of the stick should reach your chest level.

2. Place the middle of the plate on top of the stick.

3. Spread your fingers over the top of the plate.

4. Twist your wrist to make the plate spin.

5. See how long you can keep the plate spinning.

▲ *When you are ready, spin the plate by twisting your wrist.*

22

How to spin a plate with a handstick start:

1. Hold the handstick lightly at the bottom. Point it straight up.

2. Relax your arm and shoulders. Remember not to hold the stick too tightly.

3. Place the plate on the stick.

4. Move your wrist slowly in a circle. The top of the stick should also move in a circle. (The handstick makes a shape like an ice-cream cone.)

▲ *The plate should hang on the handstick like a jacket on a hook.*

23

5. Speed up your wrist motions. The stick should move along with the plate.

6. When the plate is going its fastest, quickly stop the stick in the middle of the plate.

7. Hold the stick firmly. The stick should slip into the dimple.

8. When the plate slows down, try speeding up the wrist circles again.

▲ *You are spinning a plate!*

How to do the toss start:

1. With one hand, hold the handstick straight up.

2. With the other hand, hold the bottom of the plate.

3. Spin and toss the plate up onto the stick.

4. Catch the spinning plate on the stick. Make sure the plate doesn't bounce off.

5. Stop the stick quickly. Hold the stick firmly. The stick should fit into the plate's dimple while the plate is spinning.

▲ *Toss the plate onto the stick.*

Doing Your Own Juggling Tricks

A good juggler needs many skills. You need good timing and balance. You also need to be able to throw and catch.

After you learn how to juggle three beanbags, try four, five, six, or even seven. You could also try juggling other things. Use your imagination. With practice, you can do almost any new trick.

You may juggle for fun at first. In time, you could juggle in competitions. One day, you may juggle for a living in a show or a circus. Jugglers young and old are members of juggling clubs around the world.

◀ A group of jugglers in Washington, D.C., practices outdoors.

▲ A young juggler

Glossary

drop—a failure to catch an object in juggling

handsticks—wooden sticks used to spin plates

juggling—keeping several objects in the air at the same time by tossing and catching them

pattern—the paths followed by the objects being juggled

props—the objects being juggled

run—a number of successful tosses and catches

Did You Know?

- In ancient Rome, people called jugglers "knife throwers" and "ball players."

- American actor and comedian W. C. Fields (1879–1946) worked as a comic juggler in the United States and Europe.

- The International Jugglers' Association was created in 1947. Today it has thousands of members in several countries.

- On the set of *Guinness World Records: Primetime,* on October 16, 1998, Chester Cable of Riverside, California, juggled a large table seventeen times in a row using only his feet.

Want to Know More?

At the Library

Bulloch, Ivan, and Diana James. *I Want to Be a Juggler.* Princeton, N.J.: Two-Can Publishing, 2000.

Cassidy, John, and B. C. Rimbeaux. *Juggling for the Complete Klutz.* Palo Alto, Calif.: Klutz, Inc., 1994.

Gifford, Clive. *The Usborne Book of Juggling.* Tulsa, Okla.: EDC Publications, 1995.

McGill, Ormond. *Balancing Magic and Other Tricks.* New York: Franklin Watts, 1986.

Mitchelson, Mitch. *How to Be a Juggler.* Brookfield, Conn.: Millbrook Press, 1997.

On the Web

Flying Karamazov Brothers

http://www.fkb.com/

For the biographies, history, and tour schedules of this juggling troupe

International Jugglers' Association

http://www.juggle.org/

For information about local juggling clubs and festivals

Juggling Information Service

http://www.juggling.org/

For juggling news, tips, and links

Through the Mail

International Jugglers' Association
P.O. Box 218
Montague, MA 01351
To get information about becoming a member of this juggling organization

On the Road

Juggling Festivals

http://www.juggling.org/festivals/

To get information about juggling festivals in your area

Index

About the Author
After graduating from Brown University, Elizabeth Dana
Jaffe received her master's degree in early education from
Bank Street College of Education. Since then, she has
written and edited educational materials. Elizabeth Dana
Jaffe lives in New York City.